Joel J. Pinto

A Seller? Me?

A SELLING MANUAL FOR ENTREPRENEURS

Alicante – Spain – September 2017

A Seller? Me?

A SELLING MANUAL FOR ENTREPRENEURS

ISBN-13: 978-1548062804
ISBN-10: 1548062804

www.joelpintoromero.com
Facebook: **joelpintoromero**
Twitter: **@JoelPintoRomero**
Skype: **JoelPintoRomero**
Email: **joel@joelpintoromero.com**

Edited by: Brígida Núñez / Carolina Lafuente.
Translated by: Humberto Arturo Reaza J.R

El Altet, 03195. Elche - Alicante. Spain.

Table of contents

Dedication

I give thanks to God
for having granted me the opportunity
to come this far,
for always having been on my side,
even during those times
in which I did not paid any attention to Him.

To my parents for having sown in me
the values and principles that have made me who I am,
both the good and the not so good things
about myself.

To my wife, Carolina, with whom I have learned
the real meaning of true love
and of staying united,
"in the good and in the bad,
in health and in disease".

To my kids, Daniel Alejandro and Gabriel David,
for filling my days with their joy, innocence,
and giving me enough strength
to continue fighting and moving forward.

My sons, never stop chasing after your dreams
nor striving after what you really love.

God bless you always.

Why write this book?

In many conversations I have had with colleagues and friends who have decided to start their own businesses, I realized that everything flows magnificently well, up until the point when we begin to talk about "what are you going to do to obtain your first sales?"

At this point I usually find that either they had not considered the issue of sales in depth (so they have not developed a specific plan to generate new customers), or they want to hire a person to do the sales work, while they concentrate their efforts on product development.

It is as if their business' sales were the responsibility of others and not themselves.

And why is this so, you wonder? The reason is that there are many concepts that are associated with the word "selling" which not necessarily describe the reality of the process of selling a product, and that can make more than one person feel uncomfortable.

And with the "contribution" of people such as Victor Lustig who, in 1925, found himself into what he thought was a great opportunity to make easy money and was able to convince a group of unsuspecting investors to put their money down and buy the Eiffel Tower from the French government, the issue gets a little more complicated, obfuscating the act of "selling" as if it were something that involves the using of inadequate selling strategies, or even, resorting to unethical and reprehensible ones, as Victor Lustig did.

However, selling is an activity that injects energy into the world economy. Thanks to the sale of goods and services, locally and internationally, countries grow as well as their societies.

The welfare of families increases because there are vendors who promote the purchase of products that meet a host of needs.

We have witnessed impressive progress in all areas of our daily life, thanks to the fact that, at some time and place in the world, someone has managed to sell their ideas correctly to the right person and, together, have been able to develop for us an immense quantity of products.

> *In itself, selling as such is a fundamental activity in any business, regardless of size.*

That's why in the following pages you will find, in plain language, as if we were having a face to face conversation, the explanation of various issues closely associated with the activity of selling, so you can apply them to your own business project and start the selling process in full swing.

Thank you for choosing this book, and for giving me the opportunity to share with you the product of my training and my experience, both professionally and personally.

You are an entrepreneur and ... don't like selling?

There is no person in the world who knows your product better than you: from the smallest detail, to all its features, to what makes it different from the products offered by competitors, and many other things.

Similarly, you are the only one who knows in detail where you want to take your business to, how you want it to be perceived by your customers, the image you want to develop for it, and, ultimately, the contribution you want to make to society.

As an entrepreneur and owner of your own business, no one has a capacity equal to yours to sell the product.

And it is precisely for that reason, because you know your business and product so well, that you're the one most qualified to sell it, in other words, to convince others to become involved in your project, either by contributing capital as partners, working with you as employees and collaborators, or also to attain customers who, with their purchases, support the growth of your company.

Many entrepreneurs are very good at attaining investment partners, collaborators and employees, but when it comes to getting customers to buy the product or service offered, in other words, "to hit the streets and close the sell" the issue turns out to be different for them. Why?

It is as if, suddenly, the job of getting customers were not your responsibility as an entrepreneur anymore, but instead had become others' responsibility.

What makes some people to consider making the initial contacts to get new customers something difficult, or even not even daring to do it at all?

Let me share with you a story: when I started as a salesman, at nineteen years old, my mind was full of preconceived ideas. I would consider salespeople as annoying characters, too insistent, and if at some point I dropped my guard, I was going to be convinced to buy something that I did not want, or that I even needed.

But then, after completing my academic training in advertising and marketing, and gathering some years of experience in sales, I have had the opportunity to understand many concepts and call everything by its name. Today I can recognize selling as the key element for growth, not just yours, but for any business.

I understand that the difficult part of the search for these new customers is having to knock at the door of completely unknown people and, above all, getting used to these people telling you: "no", nine out of ten times, especially when the business owner turns out to be you.

However, if we understand selling as it really is and how important it is within your overall business plan, everything becomes easier.

Selling is nothing more than an intended communication process.

If you ask me to define the word "sell", I would necessarily have to say that is a way to communicate an idea convincingly to someone else. I have an idea that I think is valuable, important or very good, and I want to convince you about my view.

It is not just simply to communicate it, but to convince, to persuade you that my idea is valid, important, and worthwhile to take it into account because it could also be good for you. I start from this conviction to want to "sell" you my idea.

The key element here is "the need to convince", of "persuading" the other person.

That is why is an intended communication, which has a specific purpose, which is different from a purely informative communication.

So ancient that we often forget its true meaning.

In the archetypical story of Adam and Eve, when the serpent convinced Eve to bite on the apple, at that very moment the art of salesmanship was born—and in that case it was simply about selling an idea. And it was so properly sold that not only did Eve eat from the apple, but also Adam, whom she invited to do the same, and the rest is a familiar story for all of us.

Thereafter, our story is full of anecdotal events that speak of ideas that were very well sold, such as that the earth was flat, or that aliens had invaded the world.

After all, these were ideas that were born in the mind of someone who was so deeply convinced that his idea was good, real, and genuine, that it necessarily had to convince, persuade their peers to think the same. And, in many cases, they managed to do so.

Is selling an inherently evil act?

While intentions are genuinely good, the act of selling is also good because here we have a person transmitting an idea to another person for the benefit of the latter. If I can convince you to stop smoking, for instance, I'm doing something good for you.

If we refer to a product or service it is the same thing. This is something that, ultimately, will be for the benefit of the recipient or buyer, or at least that is how it should be.

Now, the meaning of the word "sell" started to become tarnished when the intentions that motivated the intended communication, the sales talk, ceased to be good; when a person wanted to convince another that something was very good, when it really was not, and then resorted to unscrupulous manipulation of information, deceit or directly to lying.

And as if it weren't enough having to convince someone to purchase our product, we contemplate having to be subject to rejection almost continuously and possibly be perceived as a manipulator of information without any scruples, you easily understand why for some people the issue of "selling" becomes so complicated.

However, every day, hundreds of billions of sales are made around the world, large and small, and in most of them the intentions of the seller are good, the products do what they are supposed to do, and customers are satisfied.

And, as in many other things, we are the ones who make the difference.

Selling is not the same thing as selling one's soul to the Devil.

Some time ago I read this sentence and it got etched in my heart. Salesmanship, in itself, Is a good act, necessary for your company, for you to succeed, so you can communicate your ideas convincingly to your employees, partners, friends and clients, but it is so as long as you do not "sell your soul to the Devil".

As long as your intentions are genuine, authentic and can be communicated transparently and honestly to your audience, with nothing to hide or be embarrassed for, there is no problem.

Do not be "tempted by the Devil" and resort to dishonest tricks to convince your customer that your product is what he needs.

If at any time you notice that you begin to resort to using odd tactics to convince others of what you are saying, whether to sell an idea, a product, or your services, then you could be confusing things around and start becoming, inadvertently, in one of those characters that do so much damage to the reputation of such an important business and life activity, as it is selling.

But let's not stop here. In the following pages we will discover basic concepts on how to manage the topic of sales for your business, so it will be another area to manage productively, instead of a reason to be worried.

Start by developing your own selling skills.

If there is anything I've learned in my career is that the results we achieve are closely connected to the incorporation of certain habits in our daily routine in order to perform in an efficient manner.

Your being able to develop the ability to generate sales for your business is one of them, and it is a skill that will be fundamental to your business' growth, even if later on you will decide to outsource it or use any available alternative to get this work done for you.

I have had the opportunity to work with many professionals in the selling business and I have learned many things from them, so I can help you become better at selling and at the same time become a much more productive person for your business.

Never let the word "selling" intimidate you.

Because, as I was saying in the first chapter of this book, selling is not by itself a bad thing.

Your business and growth depend on your ability as an entrepreneur to "selling it to others" from its earliest days, even from the moment you conceive of the idea.

Either when you're going to have a meeting with a future investment partner, or when you're making your first interviews to select people who will be part of your team, or simply if you're trying to do business with a distributor that could help you develop new markets; at all times, your ability to sell your idea, your proposal, will be crucial.

Remember that there is a big difference between "selling" and "selling your soul to the Devil."

That difference is made, exclusively, by the people and the intentions that move them at the time of selling something, and it has nothing to do with the selling activity itself.

How can you develop your selling skills?

First of all, you must remember that all doors are closed until they get opened. It sounds absurdly logical, but it is a definite truth: an opportunity does not exist until you start looking for it.

It's like the story of that individual who complained against God why he had not won the lottery and the first thing God replied to him was, "My son, go out and buy your lottery ticket at least".

> *Nothing happens if we do not start moving forward. This is definitive.*

And once you have fully understood that your business growth and development depends on you, and that you should look to "open up as many doors as possible", then it is worth taking into account the following advice:

Never say "NO" to yourself.

No matter how absurd you think the proposal you have put together is, no matter how difficult the economic situation or how strong your competition is, never tell yourself you cannot achieve your goal, or that such business opportunity is not for you.

Always let the other side be the one rejecting your proposal, the one that says no. By listening to what the other side has to say, you will have a great chance to improve your proposal and grow with it. If you do not listen, how will you learn about the things you can do to improve?

Do not be afraid of rejection.

Note that for every "yes" you receive, there will be at least nine people (or more) who will tell you "no". If you always have in mind this relationship, it will be easier for you to keep the energy needed to move forward and achieve your goals, regardless of how many times you are rejected.

Remember that your business is kept alive by the people who say yes to your proposal and buy your products and services, not by those who say "no". Keep that always in mind.

Do not be afraid of making commitments.

Things made half-heartedly usually do not work out, or, if they do, they thus work out half-heartedly. You will always obtain the best results if you commit yourself to achieving them, if you do not stop searching for options and alternatives to make things happen.

Do not allow "surrendering yourself" to be an option. Always fight with all of your strength to reach your goals and, even if you did not accomplish them, you will know you have done the best of your efforts for it.

> *Remember you have to work very hard and for as long as necessary.*

Achieving the best results is always a mixture of having the required talent, working very hard, having a bit of luck and being in the right place at the right time.

From all this, the one thing under your direct control is to work very hard: devote all the time it takes to bring to a close that negotiation you so desire, to connect with your customers and develop mutually beneficial relationships. It will always pay off.

Always set for yourself great and realistic goals.

When I started riding my bicycle, I used to settle with pedaling between 20 and 25 kilometers on each trip. It was only after I decided to be more demanding with myself and setting a higher goal that I realized what I was capable of.

It was then that I exerted myself to the fullest, and I was able to reach 40, then 50 and recently 80 kilometers in one day.

Do the same: make your goal not to earn enough to live, but instead, think about earning enough money in order to live comfortably and see the difference it makes. Remember:

> *Big, realistic goals!*

Never let yourself be satisfied. Let learning and growing be always your motto.

Make every success a cause for celebration however small it may be, and as proof that you can still bring your company and your business further. No matter how difficult things are and how small are your steps forward. Make sure that they are always steps forward and see how, over time, you will have traveled an interesting path.

Do not give way to boredom.

If there is one thing I have learned in my career it is that new opportunities and customers will never stop surging, so there won't be a time" when you can really say, "This is all there is."

Feeding that spirit of continuous search for new opportunities will allow you to go far in any venture you launch, and you will always be able to achieve the best results.

Cultivate the habit of always keeping in touch.

Many deals can only be closed after many visits, and not necessarily in the first or the second one. Many products have even longer sales cycles. What if you give up too soon and stop keeping in touch with your prospective client? Well, you will simply cease to be present when he finally makes a decision to buy.

And if you are not there, what will happen? Another one will seal the deal. No tricks, nor gimmicks. Make a good follow-up for every opportunity that comes your way, let it become a habit in your work routine and never lose contact with your client, even after you have been told "no".

Focus in developing long-term relationships.

Because, after all, the best sales are made when you keep good relations with your customers. So do not focus simply on the transactions, in the sale as such — just don't!

Business deals are based on relationships, not just transactions.

Build bridges to connect you firmly with each one of your prospects and clients. Remember that the value of a customer is not only in what he can purchase from you one day, but what he can purchase over his entire life, the friends he can refer you to, and the good reputation he can create for your business.

And relationships must always be built with the intention of having them last a long, long time.

As an entrepreneur or owner of your own business, one of your main responsibilities will be always to ensuring the growth of your company, and for this you must do whatever is necessary to achieve it.

One of those required things will be to build the skills required to generate more money for the business, either by receiving instruction on how to perform the sales work by yourself, or learning to monitor and effectively manage the people who will be responsible for doing so.

Take time then to the development of your selling skills.

These tips I provided you with here will be of tremendous help in order for you to succeed but, like all things in life, it is an ongoing learning process, self-assessment and improvement, in which you are the main actor.

What can you learn from a professional salesman?

Surely you have already realized that I have developed my whole professional career in the sales area, under different names, titles and methodologies, but sales at the end of the day.

When I first started, like many people — maybe you can count yourself among them — I had my reservations about the work done by sellers.

But after more than twenty years of experience, courses, seminars, of many years being supervised and guided, and many others guiding and supervising people in my sales team, training sessions and sales presentations, I can certainly say that professional selling has given me the opportunity to build certain attitudes, which in the present time, I consider essential for anyone, both professionally and personally.

"And what are these attitudes?" You may be wondering at this time.

Do not ever be afraid of a handshake.

I remember this attitude was often called "people skills", in other words, the ability to relate to others without complexes, without prejudice, with ease and tranquility. For the professional salesman to stand before strangers and start a conversation, it is a task as natural as tying one's own shoelaces.

The professional salesperson understands that to sell a lot, he has to meet many people who may be interested in what he sells and can afford the price being requested. And so you should also understand it. You'll have to give many handshakes to meet those people who can buy your product while at the same time you develop your network.

> *A handshake is just a door that opens up and gives you a new opportunity to sell or to learn.*

And the more doors open up, the better your chances. It's a matter of pure and simple math: If out of fifty people only five buy what I am selling, then out of a hundred people ten will be purchasing what I offer them.

If I am acquainted with five hundred people, I will be making a sale to fifty. Again, pure, simple mathematics. No gimmicks and no shortcuts.

When someone says "no", learn to take advantage out of it.

Any vendor could tell you that receiving a "no" is an inherent part of their profession. In fact, when you learn to take advantage out of it, the rejection ceases to be an obstacle and becomes a great opportunity to learn more about the needs and concerns of your interlocutor, whether the latter is a client, a family member or a friend.

> *The refusal of a customer to do business with you is your best opportunity to improve the product.*

When someone tells you that he does not want to do business with you, he is saying in an indirect manner that there is something in your product, in your offer, or even in your own person, that does not work for him and that is preventing him from making a decision in your favor .

Learning to distinguish what is that "something" then becomes an opportunity to improve, to change, to grow. That "something" then ceases to be an obstacle, to become another tool in your process of growth as a company and as a person.

Always nurture the proactive search for new opportunities.

Many people believe that the goal of a salesperson is to sell more, when really selling as such, that is to say, the actual transaction, is only the result of a job well done.

Every salesperson should concentrate his efforts on the **continuous development of new business opportunities** for his company and product.

Attending to each and every one of these opportunities in a professional, coherent and efficient manner will allow you to maximize closing new sales.

> *The sale occurs as a natural consequence of a job well done. It is not an objective, but a consequence in and of itself.*

And the cycle never stops: search for new customers, close the deal, serve those new customers, and continue to seek new opportunities, close new deals and so on. A professional salesperson never stops and is continuously monitoring the market to find new opportunities.

Similarly you can do the same thing in your company.

Many businesses these days need that energy to put aside the negativity that the environment gives them and concentrate on the search for new development opportunities.

Learn how to get up after every fall, wipe the dust off and move on.

I could not tell you how many sales proposals I have prepared in my career as a professional salesman. Surely they are many, many more than I could count. And yet only a small number of them turned out to be successful at the end.

I have even submitted many proposals which I was almost certain that the result would be positive and yet, never materialized.

The business of your life, the big sale, may be just behind the next door you knock on.

I have also visited and contacted thousands of people and businesses of all shapes you can imagine. I have often been treated kindly, other times I have had doors slammed right in my face. I have met great people and also detestable characters.

However, one thing has been decisive: I have been able to cultivate the ability to get up after each failed negotiation, after every door slam in my face, after each unpleasant treatment, always with the illusion that the business of my life, that great sale which would give me a great commission, would be found just behind the next door I knocked at, the next phone call I would make, the following email I would send.

I can assure you that professional selling has taught me valuable things, some of which I have put down here for you, with the assurance that they will be useful for your business and for both your professional and personal life.

Everyone, absolutely everyone, has something to sell. Whether it be an idea, an opinion, an old utensil we have at home, or our own personhood. All of us have had to make use of our "selling" skills at some point in our lives, perhaps more than once.

Or did you not have to convince that wonderful person now living with you, that you were for her the best option that was available on the market?

That is why it is so advisable to learn these attitudes that distinguish professional sales people, the type of which always achieve good results, and put those attitudes underway in those areas of your life that you consider convenient, starting with your business.

How can you plan ahead your "cold-calling" sales?

Well, now that we are clear that "selling" is not an inherently bad activity, that as an entrepreneur is simply another task you have to do, and that there are certain things you can do to develop your selling skills, let start afoot and help you bring more sales for your business.

Let us begin with one of the most powerful tools to achieve this: "cold calling".

It is called "cold calling" simply because you are addressing, either by phone, email or the most traditional of all, door to door visits, a person who does not know you at all.

And I consider it a great tool because it helps you break free, once and forever, from the stress that stems from contacting unknown people, also offering you the opportunity to understand and control by yourself how your product is sold, and transmit this knowledge to others.

As always, let me explain myself: Let's assume that you are starting your new business and in order to get your first customers you did a flyer campaign, placed some ads in the local press, you opened your Facebook page and you have begun to follow some people in Twitter, but, despite your efforts, still no one approaches you to do business or contacts you to hire your services.

What do you do then to get new customers?

It's just at this moment when "cold calling" becomes your best ally. It is then time to go out to the street and offer the world your products or services directly, without intermediaries, face to face.

It is the best tool that exists to sell, because you control it yourself, and only you are the one responsible for the results that it can generate.

And though it seems as simple an activity as just saying: "I grab a folder with some business cards, a few very cute flyers that I just recently printed out, and hit the streets to find customers", actually "cold call" selling carries a thorough planning process if you want to perform it effectively and get its full benefits.

The "cold calling" process has 3 stages: a before, a during, and an after, in other words:

- Planning.
- The execution.
- Follow-up.

How to plan a cold calling sales campaign?

I will use as an example, by way of illustration, the sale of professional services (intangible assets), which is usually a topic a little more complicated than going out and selling a tangible product, such as those which people can feel with their own hands .

Everything that I am going to say now **should be done before you stand in front of your first door**, always remembering two things: that "the first impression is the most important" and that "there is never a second chance to make a first good impression".

We start then with the product which, in this case, is yourself. You must have it clearly defined, so you should have given a concrete answer to the following questions:

> **What are you going to offer?** What will be the extent of your services? Are you going to offer yourself as a consultant or as a "doer" of things? Are you going to offer a unique service, or will you offer several?
>
> Define with clarity the needs for which you have the capacity to provide a clear solution and how you would do so. Keep in mind that your client will not be buying your services but your ability to solve their problems. Make a list of needs that your client may have, and clearly develop the solution that you would have for each of them.
>
> **How much will you charge for your services?** Will you offer them for a fixed monthly payment for a specific amount of hours? Will you offer your services "as a package"? Will you have a minimum term contract, in other words, some kind of "permanence"?
>
> This is the million dollar question. If you do not correctly calculate right from the start what will be your price proposal, you can end up pigeonholing yourself as a "cheap" professional, or a too expensive one; so what is the fair middle-point? It will depend on the following.

Have you clearly defined your "unique selling proposition"? A "unique selling proposition" is what will differentiate you from the pile, from the rest of professionals who offer the same services as you do. Which is yours?

All your collateral materials must be ready and should clearly reflect the above points: what your product is, how much does it cost and what makes you different from others.

That is why the planning process is so important when you are setting up a door-to-door selling campaign. Can you imagine sending your brochures to be printed out only to realize that your printed material does not accurately reflect what you want to really offer?

Or that a cold-calling visit went well and your future customer looks for you on the Internet, or head over to your LinkedIn profile, or your website to know more about you, only to find that it is incomplete or poorly prepared? What impression do you think it would cause him?

The product should be clearly defined so that your potential customer can identify and understand it easily, with no room for doubt or vague interpretations.

If the client cannot identify your product with ease, it will cost him a lot of effort to understand your pricing proposal.

Defining your product, in this case the services you will be offering, is paramount to the success of your door-to-door cold calling sales.

It is very important that you know what you are offering in as much detail as possible, so you're able to answer all questions that your potential customer makes you during the visit.

Once you have defined the product, what do you think we should do then?

Who are going to be your first "cold-calling" prospects?

Ok, your product is clearly defined, your collateral material is in order, you have clear how much will you charge for your services and even had the chance to make a template in an Excel spreadsheet to calculate your pricing proposals.

The next step is obvious: go down the road to do door-to-door cold selling visits, that is, knocking on doors of people who do not know you at all, doing a presentation of your services if allowed and, in the best of cases, get them to accept your proposal and hire your services.

But is there any way to make sure the doors are not so cold during the first visits and reduce the stress of being in front of a stranger?

Well, actually there is a way—and it is far more simple than you could ever had imagined.

Door-to-door cold calling can be done in two ways: on one hand, what is defined as plain hard door-to-door cold calling, that is, knocking on doors of people who do not know you at all or, on the other hand, being a little more practical and provide some "warmth to the door", so to speak, so that they are neither so cold nor so hard the first time you knock on them.

How is it done?

Begin with your network of contacts and friends.

Surely during your professional life you have accumulated a significant amount of contacts, friends and relatives with whom you already have some type of link, regardless of how strong it may be.

What if then you start by making a list and include in it all those people who are within your current circle of contacts who might be interested in the product or services that you will be offering?

What are the advantages of starting to work on this initial contact selection?

The first advantage is obvious: since there is a prior relationship, the stress of visiting a person who is completely unknown disappears, the door will be open for you, and the visit will not be that "cold".

The second and very important advantage is that, being a person who already knows you, the presentation you are going to make of your product or services may be a little more "informal", lighter, allowing you to do it with more confidence and your acquaintance will have the opportunity, moreover, of making recommendations for you to do it even better, depending on the degree of trust between both of you.

It could be said that these visits to your network of contacts will allow you to polish your sales presentation, so that it is completely ready when the time comes for you to stand up right in front of a person who is a complete stranger to you.

And when you have already contacted all people within your initial list, how do you choose more prospects to visit?

Suppose then that you have exhausted your initial contact list, you have done all the visits you could have done to people who already knew you beforehand, and you have been able to close your first few sales.

What will you do now that you have already visited all the people that you had included in your initial contact list and you have no one else you could visit?

It is then time to create a list of new cold-calling prospects, and these are going to be people who do not know you at all for real.

To do this, there are several things you should consider so you can get the best possible results when planning your visits:

- According to whether you intend to offer your services on an international, national or local level, your prospect list will change. Define this clearly in order to utilize your time effectively. It makes no sense, at first, to travel long distances to make door-to-door selling visits if your product will only be offered locally, unless they are contacts with strong and true potential.
- Depending on the service you will be offering, then you can search the Internet for business and companies that are interesting prospects for you.
- Based on the list of companies and people you have prepared, organize thus your visits according to the geographical location of each of them, so you can make as many visits in the shortest time possible and avoid unnecessary expenses.

Once you have created a list of people to visit, it is best to do two things:

• **Document yourself whenever you can about your new prospects.** The idea here is to familiarize yourself the best you can with regard to companies you will be visiting, so you have a clearer idea of how you can better offer your services or products.

• **Getting a contact person or a reference name:** this is perhaps the most difficult goal to achieve, but always worth the effort. Try to get a name, even the assistant's or receptionist's, if necessary. It will always be much easier to step right through the door asking for someone in particular, than doing it totally blind.

And at this point, you are ready to continue doing your door-to-door sales campaign, but if you have noticed, the doors that you are knocking at are not so cold anymore, are they?

A key step for the success of any door-to-door sales campaign is to do the proper selection of the market that you are going to head towards.

If you are just starting out, it is best to always do it through your immediate network of contacts and the referrals you can get therein, because this lightens up the process by far.

If you have already reached your network of contacts and resulting referrals, then it becomes much more important to properly choose the public segment which you are going to be approaching.

As in many other things, being in front of the right person with the right product, is a key element to achieving the best results.

Always follow up on all your sales efforts.

The "follow-up" process defines the ongoing relationship you have with your customers before, during and after the actual business transaction is performed.

It refers to a commitment on your part to communicate with them effectively, not in an unilateral manner, but bilaterally, so that information flows freely, from one side to the other.

It is a relationship in which you must be willing to respond to what your customer or prospect puts on the table at all times, because this is the seed from which the business relationship between you will develop, even more so when you have understood that you are the first one to be interested in having relationships with your customers that work well and last over time.

That you're only interested in closing the sale? We all know that but, how do you know when your prospect is ready to buy?

That is why there is an important "follow-up" process: the attentive and effective listening to all activity that occurs between your company and your prospects, once you have begun the sales endeavor.

To understand the importance of "following-up", it behooves you to assume as yours the idea that your sale is on your client's side and goes back to you only when they buy your product or hire your services. But only up until that point and never before that.

If the actual purchase does not occur, the sale does not exist yet. Or could you keep your business running, without customers to buy your products? Of course not!

"Following-up" is a sales habit that you must cultivate, because it implies that you will be attentive to each and every one of the things that occur in the environment of your business and, more important still, when you start to make any kind of contact with a potential customer, either in a digital environment or a traditional way, in order to close a sale.

If you have been visiting a prospect and you have not found him at his office, for example, take note when you should be contacting him back, if there is a best time to call, if you must make an appointment, etc.

If you had the opportunity to speak with the person who makes decisions, even better yet. Take note of all the agreements made, the comments received, their feedback regarding the proposal that you submitted.

Bottom line: be sure to jot down everything that can allow you to develop a fruitful and professional business relationship with your prospect.

Have as a norm in your professional life to show interest for your customers, making the appropriate follow-up of all prospective clients you have.

Proper follow-up means you will be present at the time the customer makes the decision to purchase and, if so, you will carry out the business and not your competition.

A thorough planning, a clean execution and appropriate follow-up will be the key for your door-to-door sales campaigns to give you the chance to access many new business opportunities.

How can you recognize when a potential customer is really a good one?

A very common story that has happened to all of us who are involved in sales (and more than once, of that I'm sure) is to make a sales presentation, one of those from which you come out really satisfied, you have kept a very positive conversation with your potential customer and you exchange many and varied ideas with him.

Your prospect thanks you for all the information you have provided him, recognizes that the solution you offer him is aligned with the needs of his company, makes some questions regarding what could be the price of your offer, asks you to prepare a formal proposal and even goes over possible delivery dates and so on.

Obviously, with a big smile on your face and that wonderful feeling of having done a good job and having a new project in your pocket, you go back to the office.

You have very clear that, based upon your experience, you have received from the "future-client" green light to move forward with this project and then you sit down with your team to prepare the proposal, in accordance with everything that you talked over with the prospect.

When you are done with it, you send it to your prospect by email, or fax or by whatever method you find most convenient. You know he will be waiting for it.

When you try to contact the person again to follow up, and see what he thought about your offer and know when you may receive an approval from him, you find the most profound silence. You try again, you write him once more to get his opinion, but nothing happens.

Silence.

Never assume anything and always look for a specific answer from your potential customer.

What could have gone wrong when everything seemed perfectly aligned in order for you to close the sale? Obviously you become perplexed, stunned and confused. What did it really happen?

What happened during that meeting, which was apparently so good, but you could not see? Why does your client not return your calls now? Why does he not show the same interest he had when you last met?

Perhaps it is simply a matter of bad manners or lack of courtesy. Perhaps it is just that he has been very busy, went on vacation and forgot to let you know, perhaps he was suddenly fired from his job, or did not receive approval from his superiors to accept your proposal and is too embarrassed to tell you because he knows he has caused you to lose some very valuable time.

Maybe is none of the above.

Never assume anything or get carried away by what "you think it could have been."

Assuming things is usually dangerous when it comes to sales. When you assume you have a business deal in your pocket, you get too comfortable; you lower your guard down and tend to relax the effort you are doing to follow-up with your potential client in an adequate manner.

And the same thing happens when you assume that you lost the business deal: you close the door to your prospect and stop paying to it the attention you should. In both cases, you're making a mistake.

First of all, and in every sales presentation, you should make sure (but not in an "assumed" fashion, but by doing the corresponding questions to your prospect) of the following:

- That you have covered all of their needs and answered all their concerns.
- That the customer (or prospective client) understands the value of the proposal you are offering and the impact that such a solution will have for his business.
- That the person you are talking to has the ability and authority to make a decision.
- That you have clearly understood what is the process to be followed in order to get approval or rejection of your proposal.

If you are completely sure (again without assuming anything, but with real assuredness) you have covered all of the above, what was it then what happened?

Make your prospective client get involved and be committed to the sale process.

Be sure to make a summary of all agreements made at the end of each sales presentation or meeting (regardless of how positive it has been) and to ask if there are additional questions that must be resolved before concluding.

If all is well, then you need to make compromises: you need to establish what will you do (prepare a formal proposal, for example) and what is the part that will be performed by your prospective client (revise your proposal and give you an answer within a predetermined timeframe, for example as well).

That is, never leave a sales presentation with commitments made only on your side and none on the other side of the table.

You must, as well as them, participate in the process equally, with the understanding that the benefit is for both. If there is only commitment on your side, then your prospective client is not committed enough in the process and, therefore, you are starting to assume things that are probably not correct.

If there is no willingness to engage with you and your company in the following steps to take after the presentation, and even schedule a new follow-up meeting, it is a clear sign that he still has not bought into your proposal and thus the business deal is not yours just yet.

The best way to ensure you are on track is to confirm that your prospect is determined to go ahead with you, and that can only be achieved by having him also commit to the sales process and not allowing all the efforts it takes to be coming only from your side.

> *If your proposal is really interesting and solves the problem that the customer has, what would keep him from committing himself to you?*

Always remember that just as it is important to have many prospective clients interested in your products and services, it is equally important that these prospects are really valid ones, and not simply illusions that you have made for assuming things when you should not have done so.

Commitments must always belong to both sides.

What things can you do to increase your business and sell more?

Running a business can become for you a daunting task and overwhelm you very easily. There are so many things that you should take into account that, many times without trying, you can stop paying attention to the most important issue: **bringing in money!**

However, with the understanding that the success of your business revolves around generating sales continuously, there are many different things you can do to increase the visibility of your business and sell more.

If you don't show it, they won't buy it.

Make your business be known.

If you don't show it, you're not going to sell it. Design for it a good corporate identity, simple but with impact, with elements that differentiate you. Distribute business cards among your friends and acquaintances, among suppliers, and partners.

Let all people know what you specialize on and what you do for a living.

Take advantage of all available tools.

Tools such as email marketing, online videos, social networking and many other easily available marketing venues, allow your business to reach places where you cannot physically be present, thereby increasing its visibility and creating opportunities for people interested in what you offer to make a purchase, or at least take you into account.

Make sure you are always available either by phone, e-mail or any other channel.

So as to offer your customers advice and recommendations about your products, or even products that you do not have in your inventory, as well as to resolve any doubts or complaints that may arise after the purchase is made. Being always available is an excellent opportunity to build loyal customers, strengthen long-term relationships and generate additional sales.

Put some of your money in advertising.

It is a common mistake done by entrepreneurs to expect their business to grow in an "organic" way, with the least money investment possible. Do not make this mistake too. If you have a restricted or minimum budget, this only means you have to optimize the use you are doing of money or simply the way you are spending it, but this does not mean at all you cannot do absolutely anything.

Do some advertising, no matter how discreet it is, and through the venues that turn out to be the most convenient according to your particular situation.

Participate in or organize events within your community.

Especially those events which can directly connect you with or give support to your current, or potential customers. Not only will it help you create a strong brand presence, but will also serve to give a more humane personality to your business and its image.

Take good care of your sales and your salespeople.

Manage your sales department with goals you supervise regularly.

It does not matter whether these goals may be daily, weekly or monthly. That will depend on the sales cycle of your product. In any case, the important thing about goals is that they allow you to confirm if things are going well or whether, on the contrary, it is time to make decisions and change course.

If you are meeting your goals, set higher goals, but let them always be reasonable and realistic: one of the easiest ways to destroy a business is setting unrealistic and unachievable goals. To pretend, for example, that a business just beginning to flourish could generate enough profit to buy a corporate jet in six months is not only unrealistic but impossible.

Goals, the more real they are, the more feasible.

Empower your sales team continuously.

Only through continuous training, can your salespeople be more effective at each visit to customers or even at the counter of your shop. There are specific techniques for each case, which will surely be of interest for you.

If you do not have a sales team, seriously consider developing one for your company, no matter how small it may be as long as it is, at least, comprised by two people. The results will always be positive.

Promote healthy competition among your salespeople.

Offer your sales team rewards and incentives, help them improve their performance every day, take proper care of them and reward their achievements. A motivated and committed sales team is the bulwark of a company that maintains continuous growth, or at least keeps in constant search for new business opportunities.

It is said that "Those who have obtained a client, have gotten a treasure."

Try to get to know your customers better.

Make a sincere effort to know who your customers are, what motivated them to reach out for your business, where they live, what they like and how they heard about your business.

With all this information, prepare a complete database of your customers. And do not feel satisfied, as long as it is possible, with only collecting traditional contact information (phone, email and that kind of stuff) but also, about knowing a little about their tastes, interests and lifestyle.

All data you collect will allow you to identify positioning opportunities for your company as well as to develop more effective marketing and promotional strategies.

"The important thing is not for your customers to come in, but to always come back"

Thus you should concentrate your efforts on making your customer purchase experience a phenomenal one, that entices him to do business with you and no one else, and even give them enough reasons to recommend you to his or her friends.

Offer your customers different payment options.

Once it happened to me that I went to make a payment at a restaurant and the establishment where we were having dinner only accepted cash. I had to go to the closest bank teller and withdraw the money to pay. That was a whole lot of nuisance.

Prevent this from happening to your customers. Do not miss a sale just because you do not have the means to charge a customer who wants to pay.

Shine in the after-sales service.

Customer loyalty is born only when the product purchase has been made, so it is an excellent idea to take every opportunity to stay at his side, to be available and willing to solve any problem that may arise or just make sure that everything has gone as you and your customer expected.

It is thanks to a good after-sales service that you will begin to have opportunities to strengthen your relationship with each customer and make them loyal followers of your brand and your product.

Reward your most loyal customers.

A customer who regularly buys from you is a priceless treasure that you must pamper and keep at all costs. Invite your most loyal buyers to share their experience with others. Make them, whenever possible, ambassadors of your brand. Word-of-mouth advertising remains the most powerful promotion these days, especially in a hyper connected world like ours.

Garner the most benefit possible from each of your most loyal customers.

Do regular satisfaction surveys among your customers.

Always let them know that their opinion is important to you, and take into account what they tell you in order to make real improvements on your products and services.

A customer who feels that the company listens to what he has to say, feels deeply valued and, as a token of appreciation, will continue to reward you with his trust, purchases and recommendations.

Take advantage of local sales seasons.

During holiday seasons and special local events, your customers will be willing to buy more so your promotions will be more effective and will increase your numbers significantly.

And I think that by now you have enough ideas to put to work and increase your sales.

As you can see, all these tips represent simple things that do not take much effort to be implemented, once you realize the important influence they can have on your sales growth and the consequent development of your business.

Have them in mind when doing your business planning and put them to work according to what time and resources you have available for it, or even better if you have a group of people who can devote their time to implement them.

The only thing that can happen is that your sales start to grow and flow in a more orderly and organized manner and that is definitely good for your business.

What can you do to help your sales team be more effective?

Often it is thought that lack of motivation is the most important determinant factor in the effectiveness of a salesman or a sales team. And certainly motivation is a vital element for any seller. There is no doubt about it, and whoever does doubt this, it could be that such person does not have a clear idea regarding the actual sales process.

The reality is that selling, as such, is fundamentally an emotional act and to do it effectively a salesperson should be in an optimal emotional state. Not an excellent emotional state, as you could think, nor a "life-is-very-beautiful" kind of state. No. Just an optimal emotional state.

To be truly effective, a seller must be in an appropriate emotional state.

Can you imagine a sales representative making a presentation of your products to a group of potential buyers and that is clearly visible on his face that he is not meeting his sales target that month, and therefore will not have enough money, not even to bring food home?

Or that maybe he is going through a breakup and instead of talking to your potential client about your product he sits down to talk about the terrible things that his significant other did to him and that caused the separation?

But beyond motivation, which is always important, a salesman also needs other things to achieve his best results.

The first thing a seller needs to be more effective is proper supervision.

And supervising does not mean that you should become an all-seeing eye looking over the shoulder of your sales team twenty-four hours a day to make sure they are doing their job, visiting customers, filing reports, and so on.

No. Absolutely not.

Supervision and control are two very different things, and also generate very different results.

Supervising what your sellers are doing is a task that must be performed continuously, on a daily basis, face to face, by phone or by email, as you see fit, but you must do it at a set frequency and through any available channels.

> *Being a boss who oversees is not the same as*
> *being a boss who's a control freak.*

Only by supervising will you be able to detect when the "emotional levels" of your sales team are below what is appropriate to do the job well, and is then your responsibility as a supervisor, to take the measures necessary to increase team motivation.

But be very careful!: this is about supervising, about detecting situations that require your intervention to improve them and keep the spirits up, not that you become that kind of boss that disrupts the work of his sales team twenty times a day, without any valid reason, and just to reiterate his position as "the boss" and his need to control people's time.

The second thing that is needed is to have realistic and achievable goals.

How did you establish the sales goal you expect from your sales team? Through divine inspiration, or simply because you thought out of a number out of the blue on that day which you could (or aspired to) meet in sales during that particular period of time?

There is nothing more interesting than to sit down and talk with an entrepreneur and ask him how much money he wants to make in sales over the next year, or in the next six months. The expressions on their faces say it all: They have not even the slightest idea, or the idea they have is simply the manifestation of their own illusions, hopes, or perhaps their needs.

> *Your sales goals cannot be the manifestation of*
> *your desires, but a real and achievable number.*

A sales goal should be, first of all, realistic:

- How can your company achieve sales in that amount of money?
- What reasons do justify this?
- What were the sales for the same period last year?
- How much money are you planning to invest in advertising to boost sales during that period?
- What is your competition doing and how you plan to respond to them?

I give you an example: I go biking regularly. I started biking fifteen miles every time I went out. Today, I can get thirty or close to forty miles in one day, if I try hard enough.

Could I go a longer distance? Probably yes, but beyond sixty miles on a single ride, it would not only be unrealistic but an attempt against my own health that could have serious implications.

> *An unrealistic sales goal simply leads your sales team to frustration and, consequently, to a decrease in their performance.*

This is why a sales goal is not simply a number that one pulls off the top of one's head. There is a whole reasoning behind it.

There are many things in your performance as a company that can affect that of your sales team, so it is very important that your sales goals are realistic and achievable. Generally, and by my own professional experience, when goals are realistic, they are also perfectly achievable.

Do not try to sell yourself to your own sales team.

Your sales team does not need to have you telling them your company is the most wonderful thing that exists in the whole world, or that your products are among the favorite items for each of your customers, or that your prices are the most competitive in the whole market. Everyone says the same thing, believe me.

On the contrary, your salespeople need to be prepared with the truth, and nothing but the truth, in order to make consistent sales in the market.

> *You must provide your sales team with an honest sales training above all, and to prepare them to face a very contentious and competitive market.*

It's like going to war: If you do not tell your soldiers, with absolute clarity, what size and strength the enemy does have and how you recommend them to go about it and deal with it, you will simply be sending them to a certain death.

Can you imagine a boxer who goes into the fight thinking that his opponent's best punch is a straight right jab, when in fact it is the left hook? What an unexpected surprise will his ribs take when he feels the first punches of his opponent!

Well, the same thing happens to your sales team: they must be adequately prepared to effectively and positively deal with all the challenges that may arise in the market.

There are no bad sales people, but bad sales managers.

And this is a truth that has always been my North as a sales director: **My sales team and their performance are both my full responsibility.**

So your team performance is dropping? It is your responsibility as their immediate supervisor to analyze and find out what may be the cause and implement corrective measures.

That you have a salesperson that is really bad at selling? If he is so bad, how come you have not noticed before? Why have you not made the decision to let him go, if applicable? And if he was bad from the very beginning, why did you hire him to start with?

Managing the sales department of your business, more than just being a responsibility, is an extraordinary opportunity to bring your best effort to the growth of your project. As I said before at the beginning of this chapter:

- If you are clear in your responsibility as supervisor of your sales team, — even if you are making the sales yourself—and
- if you set clear goals that your team must meet and these goals are realistic and achievable, and
- you keep always in your mind that the performance of your team (and your own) is your sole responsibility,

Then your sales team will be properly supervised, you will be able to motivate them correctly at whatever times you find most convenient, and you will help them be more effective carrying out their job, and so they will have no problem achieving the results that you demand from them.

Can a salesperson have nothing to do at any time during his job?

Some time ago, talking with a pal of mine who was employed as a salesman for a company, just as he was returning from his summer vacation, he said that the first days in office made him extremely weary, because "he had no work to do, nothing at all."

Obviously the next question I asked was, "why do you feel you have nothing to do?" To which he replied: "The reason is that all my clients are still on vacation."

And after pondering about his answer, I realized that my partner was making the mistake that many sales representatives do: investing most of their time managing a portfolio of active clients, regardless of the turnover being obtained from it.

In this situation, one might ask the next question: "who is then in charge of seeking new customers?"

When managing your sales team, or even if you're the person in charge of carrying out the sales area of your company, you should always stay focused on which is your main task: getting new customers.

In short, two tasks: searching and managing.

The daily scenario of a sales representative for any company, medium or small, should be to divide his time between performing three tasks:

- Proactively and continuously looking for new business opportunities.
- Ensure that orders from all active customers are served in the best way possible.
- Develop relationships with all his customers, whether they are active or under development.

Of these three, probably the reason why you have hired a sales representative for your business is to be in charge of finding new customers.

However, if your business is a small one or if you are someone who thinks that a salesperson must take responsibility for all after-sale activities, such as billing customers or managing product delivery, think again, because you will be using your salespeople's time for something that is not their primary task and, eventually, this will bring its negative consequences on their performance, as it always happens whenever you put your time into doing something you shouldn't.

And if you are salesman and sometimes you find yourself in the same situation as my friend did, always keep in mind that your main task is to find new customers for the company. If "all your clients are on vacation," it is then the best time you have to find new customers, because nobody will be telephoning or e-mailing you with requests for information or consultation.

Your client portfolio must grow continuously.

And this is the task that truly is of fundamental importance for the economic success of your company. If a seller has enough free time to say that "he has nothing to do", it is then that he is not trying hard enough to get new customers for the company.

From my point of view, this is one of the errors that should never be committed by any person who engages in sales, or has the responsibility to manage a sales team: focusing solely on managing the portfolio of active clients, or those who are closer to becoming active clients, and stop looking for new customers.

Why you should always look to get more new customers?

Surely your answer is going to be something like "to make more money", "to generate more sales", "to plan the growth of the company"; and even if all of them are relatively certain, there is a deeper reason for this: to create a solid customer portfolio that does not depend solely on customers who are actually buying but always is generating new business opportunities.

Yes, that is the underlying reason: having a customer base which is growing continuously ensures your company achieves the necessary commercial strength so as to not rely solely on a big customer (or a small group of customers) in particular, to cope with unforeseen market situations (falling sales, customer closures, etc.) minimizing the impact that these unexpected situations can have on your business performance.

A strong and growing portfolio of customers, guarantees your company strength to tackle unforeseen market contingencies.

Have you ever heard of companies that have closed their doors simply because they lost a customer who represented a significant percentage of its total turnover?

Or companies that simply lost a significant portion of their market share and could not recover quickly, for not having a broad and diversified portfolio of customers?

Cases like these have been many, and are documented on the Internet. You can look them up and surely learn a lot from them, and recognize the importance your salespeople have (even including yourself if you have taken over the responsibility of selling in your own business) when it comes to continuously finding new customers and developing a strong customer base.

If you cannot find new customers, you are not looking hard enough.

Each day hundreds, if not thousands, of new consumers join the market who may become potential customers for your product or service. That is why you should not pay that much attention when people say, "the market is completely covered," or when you tell yourself that "customers for my product type belong to a very limited niche."

The one who searches with intent always finds something new. Make such search a habit for you and your sales team.

If in a general manner I had to make a list of the activities in which your sales representatives should focus their time, it could be summarized in the following four tasks:

- Manage everything related to customers who are actively buying.
- Strengthen and deepen relationships with these customers buying.
- Develop relationships with potential customers.
- Continually seek new potential clients for the company.

There is no room for a sales representative to feel idle at any time: if he is not managing active customers, he is then looking for new customers.

And if you manage a sales team which, really and honestly, is busy enough so as to not spend a greater amount of time finding new customers for your business, then these are excellent news for you: it's time to hire more salespeople!

When is the proper time to delegate the search for new customers?

If you do not really have the time to search for new customers, you must then find sales representatives who do it for you. Above all, in any sales department that wants to be considered effective, two tasks must be carried out at all times: the active search for new customers and the effective management of existing ones, those which are active as well as those in the process of becoming active.

Look at the adjectives that I've chosen to use for each: "active" search, that is, dynamic, committed, continuous and with intent; and "effective", that is, in which all efforts are concentrated on obtaining the best results.

> *Each one of them, both the management of active clients, as well as the finding of new customers, has its own importance within the development of your business.*

Thus, in any sales venture, whether it is comprised of one or fifty people, the main objective is to attract new customers for the company.

If the time comes in which enough time is not being dedicated to attracting new customers, you seriously need to consider giving additional support to your sales team and find people who can take care of customer management related tasks.

This will allow you to regain balance on how they distribute their work and devote as much time as possible to search for new opportunities and generating new customers for your business, leaving the purely administrative tasks assigned to people specifically trained for it.

Never let your business sales to depend on a single representative.

In the chapter entitled **"Things that you can do to sell more"**, I briefly mentioned that the sales department of your company, or your sales team, always should be composed of at least two people. Never just one but always two whenever possible.

The reasons for this are many and I would like to share with you the ones that, personally, I consider most important.

Let me start by sharing with you a story that happened to a dear friend, who owned a small local business, whom I will refer to, from now on, as Mike.

> *It turns out that Mike had a sales representative, whom I will call Dick, who was supposedly a very loyal employee and had been visiting customers from the company's database.*
>
> *Dick was in charge of finding new customers, managing new orders from existing customers, writing sales proposals, following-up by telephone with all the people he visited; in brief, the normal tasks of any sales representative.*
>
> *The problem was that my friend Mike, for lack of time and perhaps a little comfort on his side, did not involve himself too much in the management of customer relationships and sales, other that ensuring the timely dispatch of merchandise.*
>
> *And since Dick was a "trusted" employee, Mike did not pay attention to Dick's performance and concentrated only on what he thought would be good enough: the numbers. If Dick was bringing in more business, it was all good; if he was bringing in less, they both would try to come out with a way to increase the numbers. Solely focusing on the numbers.*
>
> *One day, Mike had to travel and leave the country for a while and when he returned he came across the very unpleasant surprise that his "trusted" salesman, Dick, had left the company, taking all customer information with him and, as if that were not enough, he had started a small business located a few blocks away, from where he started to steal customers away from Mike.*

What are the lessons we can learn from this story?

First of all, your business depends on sales.

Do not flee away from managing your sales because it will not be good for business. This real-life story shows in a simple way the first reason why you should never give up your responsibility as a business owner and let sales management in the hands of a single salesperson, no matter how "trusted" that person could be.

Get involved! It is your duty to monitor, effectively and closely, how the money that keeps your company alive is generated, whether you do the selling yourself or you have a team of salespeople who do it in your stead.

I know many entrepreneurs tend to put aside the sales management area in their businesses because they think it can become a very stressful and tedious activity—and it could. However, here is an example of why you shouldn't do it and what might be the consequences if you put the area aside.

For how long had Dick been visiting Mike's clients telling them he was going to become independent from the company he worked for and that he would be contacting them again when he did so?

How many times did Dick stay home, saying he was visiting clients, when he was really investing his time in the preparation of his independent project?

The sales management of your business should not be measured only by sales volumes. There are many things you should take into account.

Mike will never know because he focused his sales management in sales volume alone, not paying any attention to all the daily activities that must be carried out to achieve those sales volumes.

Behind each sale, there is a process, a number of things that happen: visits, phone calls, emails, preparation and submission of proposals, following up with contacts, etc. These activities should be under your supervision. Call your customers on the phone, make sure they are well taken care of, that all is going well.

Do not leave everything up to the sales guy especially if you have only a single sales representative, even if he has your whole trust.

But let us not stop here; there are still things to share.

You should always have a substitute ready in case your sales representative must be absent.

And that is why I said it would be advisable that you had at least two people in your sales team. Have you noticed that in football games, or any sport for that matter, there are always players on the bench, ready to replace anyone who is injured during the game?

For it is a strategy that is well suited for the sales management of your business.

Here you should keep in mind that if the only person whom you have entrusted doing your business sales, gives you a call one day letting you know he got into an accident and cannot go to the office, do you have in your roster a person ready, properly prepared, and trained to replace your sales immediately without suffering an unnecessary drop in sales?

Always think about what you will do if your only salesperson leaves the company. Do you have the means to replace that person quickly?

I know we're talking about an extreme situation here, but situations like this happen, and much more often than we think. If not, look at what happened to my friend Mike.

Can you imagine a football match where you have to stop the game, because there is no one to replace the goalkeeper who fractured his ankle?

Supervise, supervise and supervise. And then, continue supervising.

And this is the point that causes more discomfort to many entrepreneurs: sales supervision—sitting down with your sales team asking them how things have gone and hearing their stories and anecdotes all the while only really wanting from them is to make their sales and not come up with tall tales.

Well then let me tell you that from those "salespeople's stories and anecdotes" you can get a lot of information about things that will help you manage your business sales in a much more efficient way, if you really listen carefully.

Listen carefully to what your salespeople have to say, and you will discover many important things for your business.

In fact you can discover new business and product development opportunities, listening to what your salespeople have to say about the market that buys your products and what's happening in it. Keep in mind always that people in your sales team directly listen to the voice of the most important part of your business: customers who buy your products and services.

You must make a sincere effort to tune up the sales management of your business and look at it from a closer point, giving it the importance it really has within your project as a whole. After all, the sales department is the one that generates the money that pays all business's costs, right?

What should you know about sales and why?

So far we have covered the main aspects that I believe every entrepreneur should know about sales. Now, it is well worth to go over the reasons why this is so important to you as well as your business development and its long term permanence.

Imagine for a moment that you had a very interesting business idea, and all the people whom you have shared it with consider it a great one with a lot of potential.

You invested time, money, and have made every effort to bring your idea to light. Finally, when everything seems to be ready, you have to put a stop to the project because you do not know what to do to get your first paying customers.

Or you do know what you have to do but feel that going out and talking to strangers is not for you, and then decided your best option is to hire a person to do the work for you.

How will you know then if the person of your choice is doing a good job or not? How can you assess their performance if you yourself do not know how to sell your own product?

By knowing how it is done, you will be able to supervise others effectively.

If you are a person who is familiar with selling, you feel at ease interacting with your customers keeping your eyes open always looking for new opportunities for your business and not stopping at anything, awesome.

When the day comes for your business to grow and you must hire someone to make the selling for you, you will be knowledgeable enough to effectively monitor their work, tell them the things they should do and not do, helping them as well to get the best result from their time and effort.

> *By knowing how to sell your own product, you can guide others on how to effectively do the selling.*

You know very well that customer relationships, handling objections, price revisions, comments that customers make about the product or services you offer, all of them provide you with valuable information for planning sales and marketing activities, and it is also valuable information you can use when providing an adequate training to future sales representatives that will be working for you.

If it were the case that you do not have any knowledge or experience about sales, then it would be interesting for you to hire an experienced sales person for your project, teach him everything necessary regarding your product and how you think it might be presented for selling, and then learn from that person how it is done.

You could then take this opportunity to learn from a professional the techniques that are frequently used, as well as the sequence that must be followed to go from the initial moments of a sales presentation to closing the deal. You'd be amazed!

That is why it is so important that you, as an entrepreneur and business owner, get yourself involved in the sales area of your project, even if it is only to acquire the necessary knowledge to supervise the team that would be responsible for doing the work thereafter.

By knowing how to do it yourself, you eliminate being dependent on a third party.

Do you remember the case I mentioned in **"Never let your sales depend on a single sales representative"**?

Well, it is an extreme case of what could happen in your sales department: the only person who is doing the sales job suddenly leaves you alone and goes to work for another company, or even a competitor. What do you do at a time like that?

Knowing that your sales are not dependent on a single person will give you a lot of peace of mind.

Definitely it is very important that you have the ability to take control of your business sales in a situation like this, get in contact with your most important customers and keep all pending orders running smoothly, so that the absence of a member (in this case, the one member) of your sales team does not become a total disaster for your business.

That is why I was also recommending you to keep your sales team always composed of at least two people: in case of the fortuitous absence of any of them, the second could take his place immediately.

If, in your case, your sales team is comprised by only one person, then consider getting yourself truly involved in managing your sales, so that any fortuitous situation like this one does not take you by surprise.

Individuals with the sales mindset are always looking for new business opportunities.

One of the main features I've found in most people who are engaged in sales is that they have a knack for seeing things from a positive point of view, trying to always find new opportunities, relentlessly, until achieving the goals that have been proposed.

As a rule of thumb, most good sellers are tireless fighters. And having such energy is always good.

It is an energy that can certainly be of much help to navigate through the sometimes tortuous path of entrepreneurship.

You should know it from your own experience: moving forward one's own business has a number of challenges that can test the temperance of your character, your patience and, in most cases, your ability to get up and keep on going again and again, standing up after every fall.

Having the ability to see all situations from a more positive note, trying to learn from each one of them is, definitely, a skill well worth cultivating.

And that is a capacity that I've been able to find in many of the top professional sellers whom I've worked with during my career, as well as entrepreneurs like you who have decided to pursue their dream and have developed a business around it.

There is a phrase that will surely be useful for you and with which we can summarize this attitude that more clearly resembles the sales spirit: "Your biggest sale, that which will generate the commission you've hoped for so much, may be just around the corner".

And some additional thoughts to wrap it all up:

To further deepen your sales training, if you already have it, or soaking up the fundamental concepts that I have outlined for you in this book (if you have some previous training), could only add a positive value to your professional and personal performance, regardless of what specific area you are in charge of within your project.

Having the ability to communicate your ideas to others in a convincing manner, with strong arguments and good intentions, also having the habit of following up on your tasks to ensure the achievement of the best results, are all skills that allow you to be a better leader, a better boss and a better entrepreneur, in every place and time.

Always remember that selling is the activity that gives life to any project or venture, and learning how to sell and how to manage the sales area of your business will be a skill that will allow you to always achieve the best performance, both your own personal performance as well as that of the sales team you have hired for your business, if you only need to act as the supervisor.

In either case, the concepts we have reviewed throughout this book will always be useful. It is my promise.

"The optimist person sees opportunity in every danger; the pessimist sees danger in every opportunity."

Winston Churchill

www.ingramcontent.com/pod-product-compliance
Lightning Source LLC
Chambersburg PA
CBHW071250170526
45165CB00003B/1288